Qatar

2022 World Cup

The Perfect Guide to this Year's World Cup Tournament

Introduction

This year's world cup promises to be one of the best ever, taking place in the desert for the first time.

It's a unique one and for some may be overwhelming, so I came up with this book where I gather information about the World Cup 2022 and put them all together in it, therefore, helping you get all the necessary informations that you need concerning the Qatar 2022 World Cup.

Go ahead of the world into this year's world cup and get the required information you need concerning it.

The stadia that will be used

The hotel around

Places that must be visited while at Qatar

And other juicy tid-bits on the participating nations

The World Cup 2022 is going to take place in Qatar from November 20 to December 18; a total of 32 teams(representing 32 nations) compete in eight groups.

It kicks off in Qatar on Sunday November 20 at the Al Bayt Stadium when the hosts take on Ecuador in Group A.

The final will be played at the Lusail Stadium in Doha a week before Christmas on Sunday December 18, 2022.

The eight(8) groups with the teams in each group are:

Group A: Qatar, Ecuador, Senegal, Netherlands

Group B: England, Iran, USA, Wales

Group C: Argentina, Saudi Arabia, Mexico, Poland

Group D: France, Australia, Denmark, Tunisia

Group E: Spain, Costa Rica, Germany, Japan

Group F: Belgium, Canada, Morocco, Croatia

Group G: Brazil, Serbia, Switzerland, Cameroon

Group H: Portugal, Ghana, Uruguay, South Korea

The venues for this year's legendary world cup?

The games will take place across eight stadia: Al Bayt Stadium, Khalifa International Stadium, Al Thumama Stadium, Ahmad Bin Ali Stadium, Lusail Stadium, Ras Abu Aboud Stadium, Education City Stadium, Al Janoub Stadium.

The Al Bayt Stadium

The Al Bayt Stadium located in Al Khor, Qatar beautiful stadium structured like tents, and is one of few stadiums with a retractable roof.

It has a carrying capacity of 60,000 and has been recorded to have carried 63,000+ before(in 2021).
This stadium is to host the opening match for the World Cup Qatar.

The Al Bayt Stadium

The Khalifa International Stadium

The Khalifa International Stadium located in Doha, Qatar is a stadium with multiple purposes.

It is a part of the Doha Sports City Complex. This Stadium has received a four star rating from the Global Sustainability Assessment System(GSAS); it is the first in the world to be aware this rating.

It has a carrying capacity of 42,000+. It is also known as the National Stadium.

The Khalifa International Stadium

The Al Thumama Stadium

The Al Thumama Stadium located in Al Thumama, Qatar is a stadium with a sitting capacity of 40,000+. It is just 12km away from Doha and is pretty close close the Hamad International Airport, making it easy for the fans to reach.

The stadium has being awarded the MIRIM/Architectural Review Future Project Award in the Sports and Stadiums category.

The Al Thumama Stadium

The Ahmad Bin Ali Stadium

The Ahmad Bin Ali Stadium located in Al Rayyan, Qatar is a multipurpose stadium but is used for football matches currently. The Ahmad Bin Ali Stadium has a seating capacity of 44,000+.

It is known popularly as Al Rayyan Stadium.

The Ahmad Bin Ali Stadium

The Lusail Iconic Stadium

The lusail iconic stadium located in Lusail, Qatar is the biggest stadium in Qatar with a sitting capacity of 80,000.

it is owned by the Qatar Football Association, and is located about 23km north of Doha.

The Lusail iconic stadium is to host the final game of the 2022 World Cup.

The Lusail iconic stadium

Stadium 974

Stadium 974 formerly known as Ras Abu Aboud Stadium is located in Ras Abu Aboud, Doha, Qatar.

This stadium is quite unique in the sense that it is a temporary venue that incorporated 974 recycled containers into the constructing of the stadium; it is a temporary venue in the sense that it will be dismantled after the 2022 World Cup.

Located and construction on a waterfront site and situated on an artifical promontory, it is a very beautiful stadium with a capacity of 40,000.

It also has received a four star rating from Global Sustainability Assessment System(GSAS).

Stadium 974

Education city stadium

Education city stadi located in Al Rayyan, Qatar is a stadium located with several university campuses at the Qatar Foundation's Education City.

A really unique stadium that glitter like a diamond as the sun passes over it earning it a nickname "diamond of the desert." It has a received a five star rating Global Sustainability Assessment System (GSAS) rating.

It has a capacity of 40,000+.

Education City Stadium

Al Janoub Stadium

Al Janoub Stadium formerly known as Al Wakrah Stadium is a located in Al Wakrah, Qatar also has a retractable roof football stadium.

A beautiful stadium that looks like a flower opening bloom in early summer is located 22km south of central Doha and has a capacity of 40,000.

The Al Janoub Stadium

Hotels around

No matter how much we love football, I really doubt that we are going to sleep at the gate of the stadium(s)...yeah, I really doubt.

So, yeah, we need to know the good hotels around the stadiums the matches will be played.

These are few of the many around that are really nice and have affordable packages:
- Mövenpick Hotel West Bay Doha
- Hilton Doha
- Al Najada Doha Hotel by Tivoli
- Al Messila, a luxury Collection Resort & Spa, Doha.
- Centara West Bay Hotel & Residence Doha
- Swiss-Belinn Doha
- Premier Inn Doha
- Aleph Doha Residences
- La Ligale Hotel, Doha

- Somerset West Bay Doha
- Holiday Inn Doha — The Business Park, an IHG Hotel.
- Double Tree by Hilton
- Millennium Hotel Dogs
- Hyatt Regency Oryx Doha
- Al Najada Doha Hotel Apartments by Oaks.
- Hilton Doha The Pearl Hotel & Residences
- Raddison Blu Hotel, Doha
- Sheraton Grand Doha Resort & Convention Hotel
- Steingenberger Hotel, Doha
- Four Seasons Hotel, Doha
- The Pearl —Doha
- Intercontinental Doha Beach and Spa
- Ezdan Hotel
- Mandarin Oriental
- Banana Island Desert Doha

This are some of the few out of very many

Tourist Attractions In Qatar

Rich in culture and happy to show the world, there is a vast array of attractions that should be visited by you while in Qatar.

- Souq Waqif
- Katara Cultural Village
- Villaggio Mall
- Grand Mosque, Qatar
- Dhow Harbour
- MIA Park, Qatar
- Imam Muhammed bin Abdulwahhab Mosque
- Falcon Souq
- Sheikh Faisal Musuem
- City Center Doha Mall
- Msheireb Musuems
- Barzan Towers
- Film City - The Mystery Village Of Qatar
- Doha Corniche

Those are places that you should visit while at Qatar.

But there are also things that you should do when there is no game going on...trust me when I say that they are worth evry bit of your time

- Doha Safaris and Wildlife Activities
- Doha keep and 4WD Tours
- Doha Outdoor Sports
- Doha Nature and Paranormal
- Doha cruises

You can take part of these activities and much more.

The Facts of the Participating Country

The participating countries(national team) past performances in the FIFA world cup

Qatar

Qatar national football team has never qualified for any single FIFA World Cup since the country's independence at 1971. While Qatar has been a regular participant in the continental AFC Asian Cup, the national side has always fallen short in the final stage of World Cup campaigns. By hosting the 2022 FIFA World Cup and its failure to qualify for the 2018 FIFA World Cup held in Russia, Qatar became the second nation after Italy in 1934 FIFA World Cup to play in World Cup without qualifying for it

But being the host of the world cup, there is a great advantage in the sense that there is morale and courage since they are literally home throughout the world cup and the fact that majority of the fans in the stadium during their game play will be theirs...and there is a special effects fans give to their team.

Ecuador

Ecuador national football team has had 4 apperances in the FIFA World Cup and had their first appearance in 2002, although they didn't accept the invitation to attend the inaugural FIFA World Cup that was held in Uruguay. They have had their best performance in the 2006 World Cup where they got eliminated during the round of 16.

They will be playing with the host country team in the opening match this 2022 World Cup.

Senegal

Senegal national football team is operated by the Senegalese Football Federation. Senegal has appeared in the World Cup only twice; reaching the quarter-final on their debut in the World Cup 2002 and getting eliminated in their second appearance which was in 2018.
But their 2022 appearance will make it the 3rd time they are qualifying for the World Cup.

Netherlands

Netherlands national football team is operated by the Royal Dutch Football Association.
Netherlands have appeared 10 times in the FIFA World Cup, reaching the finals three(3) times but not carrying the cup.

They are considered widely as one of the best national teams in world football and widely regarded as one of the greatest national teams of all time.

England

England national football team is controlled by the Football Association(FA) They have appeared in the FIFA World Cup 16 times and have carried the World Cup trophy once in the year 1966.

This present World Cup appearance will make it their 17th time of participating in the FIFA world cup game.

Iran

Iran national football team is controlled and governed by the Football Federal Islamic Republic of Iran(FFIRI).

Iran was the highest-ranked football team in Asia making them the only time that a team will hold such position for that period of time.

Iran has appeared in the FIFA World Cup Six(6) times including this recent one in the 2022 World Cup, but has never made it past the group stage.

USA

USA national football team known as The United States men's national soccer team(USMNT) is controlled bu the United States Soccer Federation
The USMNT has appeared Eleven times in the FIFA World Cup and had their best performance in the year 1930 where they took 3rd position.

Wales

Wales national football team is controlled by the Football Association of Wales which is the third oldest football association in the world, founded in 1876.
Wales national football team has appeared only twice in the FIFA World

Cup with 1958 being the first time and 2022 being the second time.

In their appearance in 1958 they made I to the quarter-final of that World Cup.

Argentina

Argentina national football team is administered by the Argentine Football Association(AFA).

The team has appeared 18 times and has gotten to the finals five(5) times including the first final in 1930, carrying the Cup 2 times in 1978 and 1986.

Saudi Arabia

The Saudi Arabia national football team is administered by the Saudi Arabian Football Federation.

The team is considered one of Asia's most successful national teams. They have qualified for the World Cup on six(6) occasions since their debut at the 1994

World Cup tournament, and reached the round of sixteen(16) in that same year's tournament.

Mexico

Mexico's national football team is governed and controlled by the Mexican Football Federation.

The team has qualified to the FIFA World Cup seventeen(17) times and has qualified consecutively since 1994; one of the six countries to do so.

Twice the team has reached the quarter-final and has been eliminated there, and this happened in 1970 and 1986; both were on Mexican soil.

Poland

Poland's national football team is controlled by the Polish Football Association (PFPN). They have qualified for the FIFA World Cup eight(8) times with the first being in the year 1938.

Twice they have won the bronze medal which were in the year 1974 and the year 1982.

France

France national football team is controlled by The French Football Federation also known as FFF.

The team has participated in the world cup sixteen(16) times.

They have won the World Cup twice 1998 and 2018, gotten 2nd position once in 2006 and have gotten third position twice in 1958 and 1986.

They are regardless as one of the best team in world football and are ranked 4th currently in the FIFA ratings.

Australia

Australia national football team is governed by Football Australia; the official governing body for soccer in Australia

The team is officially nicknamed the Socceroos.

They have appeared six(6) times in the World Cup and have had their best performance in the year 2006 where they got eliminated in 2006

Denmark

Denmark national football team is controlled by the Danish Football Association(DBU).

The Danish national football team has appeared six(6) times and have had their best performance in the year 1998 where they reached the quarter-finals of that year's world cup.

Tunisia

The Tunisia national football team is governed by the Tunisian Football Federation. They are known also as the Eagles of Carthage.

The team has qualified for the FIFA World Cup six(6) times but have never gotten past the group stage at any time.

Spain

Spain national football team is governed by the Royal Spanish Football Federal. They have qualified and participated in sixteen(16) FIFA World Cup and have won the cup once in the year 2010. They have consistently qualified for the World Cup since 1978.

Costa Rica

Costa Rica national football team is administered by the Costa Rican Football Federation(FEDEFUTBOL). They have qualified six(6) times and have reached the quarter-final once in 2014.

Germany

Germany national football team is governed by the German Football Association.

They are one of the most successful team in world football having won the world cup four times in the 1954, 1974, 1990, 2014, second (2nd) position four times and third (3rd) position four times also.

They have qualified for the World Cup 20 times.

Japan

Japan national football team Is controlled by the Japanese Football Association (JFA).

They are recognized as one of the most successful team in Asia. They had their debut in the FIFA World Cup in 1998 and since then have been qualifying for the

World Cup. They have gotten to the round of 16 three(3) times in 2002, 2010, and 2018.

Belgium

Belgium national football team is governed and controlled by the Royal Belgian Football Association. They have appeared in 14 World cup games and have had their best performance in 2018 where they took 3rd position.
They are currently ranked 2nd in the FIFA ratings.

Canada

Canada national football team (CanMNT) is controlled by the Canadian Soccer Association. They have appeared only twice in the FIFA World Cup in 1986 and 2022 and in 1986 didn't get past the group stage.

Morocco

Morocco national football team is controlled by the Royal Moroccan Football Federation also known as FRMF.

They have qualified for the World Cup six(6) times and have had their best game in 1986 where they got elimination in the round of 16.

The team is nicknamed "the Atlas Lions."

Croatia

Croatia national football team is controlled by the Croatian Football Federation(HNS).

They have qualified for the world cup six(6) times and have had their best game in 2018 where they finished 2nd and also provided the tournament best player.

Brazil

Brazil national football team is administered by the Brazilian Football Association (CBF). They are the most successful team in the FIFA World Cup tournament having won the cup five(5) times in 1958, 1962, 1970, 1994, 2002. They are the only team that has played in all the World Cup edition without any absence.

They have qualified for all the 22 FIFA World matches.

Serbia

Serbia national football team is controlled by the Football Association of Services. They have qualified 12 times for the FIFA World Cup, and have had their best play in 1930 and 1962 where they finished fourth(4th).

Switzerland

Switzerland national football team is governed by the Swiss Football Association. The country have hosted the World Cup before where they got eliminated in the quarter-final which was in 1958. They reached the quarter-final consecutively in 1934 and 1938.S national football team (German: Schweizer Fussballnationalmannschaft, Italian: Nazionale di calcio della Svizzera, French: Équipe nationale suisse de football, Romansh: Squadra naziunala da ballape da la Svizra) represents Switzerland in international football. The national team is controlled by the Swiss Football Association.

Cameroon

Cameroon national football team is controlled by the Federation Camerounaise de Football. The team has qualified eight(8) times for the FIFA world cup in 1982, 1990, 1994, 1998, 2002, 2019, 2014 and 2022, more than any other African team. They were also the first African team to reach the quarte-final of the FIFA world cup which was in 1990; that also was their best performance on the tournament.

Portugal

Portugal national football team is controlled by the Portuguese Football Federation (FPF). They played for the first time in the FIFA world cup in 1966 and in that same year had their best performance where they finished 3rd in the tournament.

Ghana

Ghana national football team is governed by the Ghana Football Association. They are nicknamed the Black stars.

They have qualified for the world cup 4 times including the 2022 world cup. They had their best play in the 2010 World cup where they got to the quarter-final of that year's tournament.

Uruguay

The Uruguay national football team is governed by the Uruguayan Football Association. They have qualified for the FIFA world cup fourteen (14) times and have won the cup twice (in 1930 and 1950). They are commonly referred to As Last Celeste (The Sky Blue).

South Korea

South Korea national football team is governed by the Korea Football Association. They are the most successful Asian football team. The have participated in ten FIFA world cup, nine being consecutive. They have co hosted the World Cup before.

This FIFA World Cup 2022 promises to be one of the most exciting and interesting World Cup ever as we see different countries with talents and quality coming together for this year's world cup.